GIFTS, CARDS
WRAPS

GIFTS CARDS WRAPS

By:
Liz Wilmes
Dawn Zavodsky

Art:
Chris Palm

A BUILDING BLOCKS Publication

COVER CONSULTANTS:
    Pat and Greg Samata
    Samata Associates, Inc.
    Dundee, Illinois 60118

CALLIGRAPHY:
    Julie Ford

PUBLISHED BY:
    BUILDING BLOCKS
    38W567 Brindlewood
    Elgin, Illinois 60123

DISTRIBUTED BY:
    GRYPHON HOUSE, Inc.
    P.O. Box 275
    Mt. Rainier, Maryland 20712

ISBN 0-943452-06-6
$7.95

Dedicated to

. . . all of those children who enjoy making and then giving gifts to people they love.

CONTENTS

SPRING

SUMMER

LOOK WHAT ELSE

SNACK TRAY

MATERIALS:

Blunt-tipped yarn needle
Styrofoam meat tray (no larger than 6″×8″)
Rug yarn
Pumpkin seeds
Water
2t salt
Bowl
3-4T butter
Plastic bag

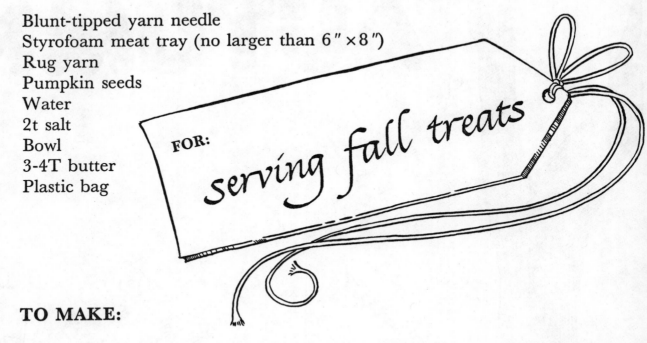

TO MAKE:

1. Using your needle, poke holes about one half to an inch apart around the edge of the meat tray.

2. Tie the yarn into the first hole in the tray.

3. Sew around the tray going in and out of each hole. Tie off the yarn.

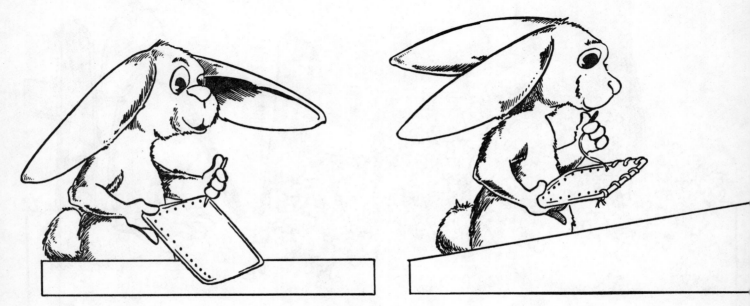

Prepare some roasted pumpkin seeds: Save the seeds from your pumpkin. Rinse them. Put them in a bowl. Cover them with water and add the salt. Soak the seeds overnight. Drain. Melt the butter. Mix the seeds in the melted butter. Spread them on a cookie sheet. Sprinkle a little salt on the seeds. Bake them at 250°, stirring them every 15 minutes until brown. Let them cool on a paper towel.

4. Put the seeds in a plastic bag and lay it on the snack tray. Secure the bag of pumpkin seeds to the tray with a piece of your rug yarn. Duplicate the recipe card and attach it to the tray.

FALL SUNCATCHER

MATERIALS:

Coffee filter (about 6-7 inches in diameter)
Water soluble markers
Bowl of water
Electric iron (optional)
Colored paper plates
Scissors
Glue
Fall colored pipe cleaners
Paper punch

FOR: *sprucing up your windows*

TO MAKE:

1. Fold the coffee filter into thirds. (See diagram.)

2. Using colored markers, color both sides of the filter.

3. Dip one of the points of the filter into the water and watch it seep across the filter. Repeat with the other two points. Let it dry overnight.

4. Open it up and smooth it out. (Optional: Iron out the creases with a cool iron.)

5. Frame the filter by cutting out the center of a colored paper plate and gluing the filter to the back of the plate.

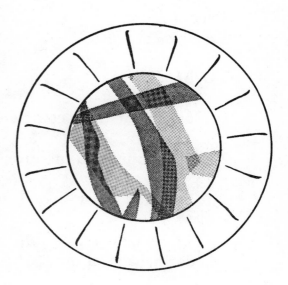

6. Make a hanger for the suncatcher by cutting the pipe cleaners in half and forming a chain with the pieces.

7. Punch a hole in the paper plate and attach the chain.

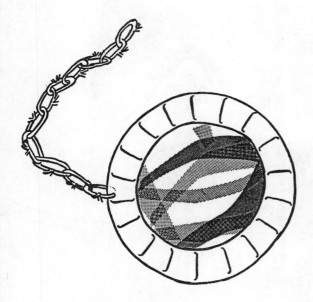

8. Hang it in a sunny window.

PUMPKIN SOAPS

MATERIALS:

Newspaper
Large bowl
1 cup water
Food coloring
4 cups Ivory Snow®
Waxed paper
Pencil
Small meat tray

FOR: *washing your hands before dinner*

TO MAKE:

1. Cover your table completely with newspaper.

2. Make your soap mixture:

   - Pour the Ivory Snow® in a bowl.

   - Add yellow and a little red food coloring to the water until you get a dark shade of orange.

   - Pour the colored water into the bowl.

   - Blend the mixture with your hands.

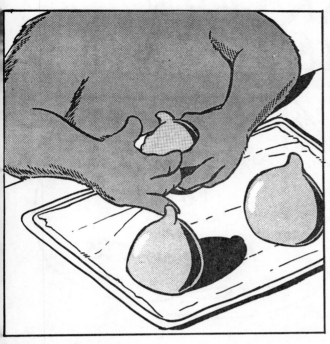

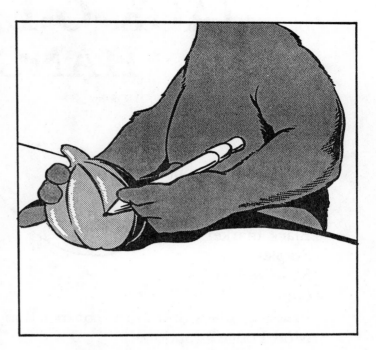

3. Cut a large piece of waxed paper to work on. Divide the soap mixture into approximately ten balls and form them into pumpkins.

4. Use a pencil to make lines in the pumpkin while it is still soft.

5. Leave on the waxed paper to dry. (The pumpkins will set up quickly but they will take overnight to dry thoroughly.)

6. Use a small meat tray for your soap dish and set one or more pumpkin soaps on it.

FOR ME?

JACK-O-LANTERN HANGING

MATERIALS:

Stack of newspaper
Orange tempera paint
Paint brush
Black marker
Stapler
Scissors
Glue
Pieces of black and green construction paper
Mod Podge® (optional)
Paper punch
Piece of heavy twine (1-2 feet)

FOR: *greeting your guests*

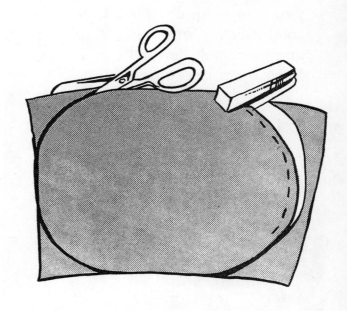

TO MAKE:

1. Open three sheets of newspaper. Stack them together. Paint the top sheet orange. Let it dry.

2. Fold the stack of three papers in half so the orange paper is facing out and the fold line is on the bottom.

3. Draw a large pumpkin outline on one side of the newspaper. Staple along the inside edge of the pumpkin leaving the top open. Cut the pumpkin along the line.

4. Add facial features with black construction paper. (Optional: Paint it with Mod Podge®. Let it dry.)

5. Crumple several additional pieces of newspaper and stuff your jack-o-lantern.

6. Add a green stem and staple it closed.

7. Punch a hole on each side of the stem and tie a piece of twine through the holes to form a handle.

TURKEY NAPKINS

MATERIALS:

Paper towels
Styrofoam meat tray (approximately 6″ × 8″)
Tempera paints
Brayer
Open turkey cookie cutters
Paper napkins

FOR: *your Thanksgiving Dinner table*

TO MAKE:

1. Make a stamp pad:
   - Cut six to eight pieces of paper towel to fit in the meat tray.

   - Pour a little tempera paint on the paper towels and spread it out with your brayer.

COLOR TEMPRA

"The paper towels need to be thoroughly soaked but not soggy."

2. Ink the cookie cutter by pressing it onto the stamp pad, and then print the turkey design on the folded napkin.

3. Repeat Step 2 to print as many napkins as you want. (If the prints become light or the stamp pad starts to dry, add a little more paint.)

4. Let the napkins thoroughly dry.

5. Stack and wrap them. You might want to use the handprint envelope. (See 'Wraps' section.)

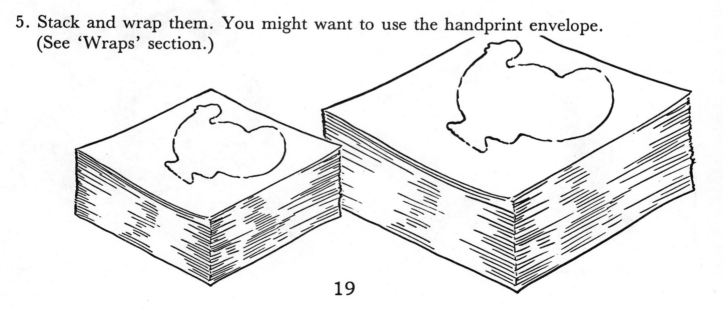

19

HALLOWEEN GREETING

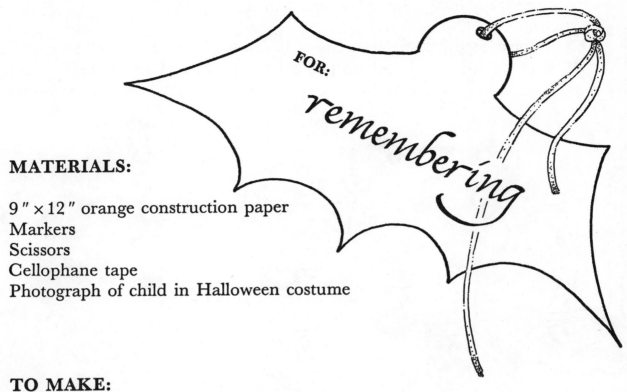

FOR:

remembering

MATERIALS:

9″×12″ orange construction paper
Markers
Scissors
Cellophane tape
Photograph of child in Halloween costume

TO MAKE:

1. Fold the construction paper in half to form a card.

2. Draw the outline of a pumpkin on the front page of the card.

3. Form the card into a pumpkin shape by cutting through both pages along the pumpkin outline.

4. Cut a window large enough for the photo to show through in the front page of the card.

5. Tape your Halloween photograph to the back of the front page so that it peeks through the opening.

6. Write your Halloween message on the inside page. (Here's a suggestion: ''Happy Halloween'' from your favorite cat, cowboy, or whomever.)

THANKSGIVING CARD

FOR:

saying "Hello" at Thanksgiving

MATERIALS:

Construction paper
Medium grade sandpaper
Turkey pattern (cookie cutter works well)
Pencil
Scissors
Ground cinnamon
Glue
Markers
Envelope
Postage stamps

"If you're putting it in an envelope for mailing, be sure the card fits the envelope you have."

TO MAKE:

1. Fold a piece of construction paper in half to form a card.

2. Trace and cut out a turkey from sandpaper.

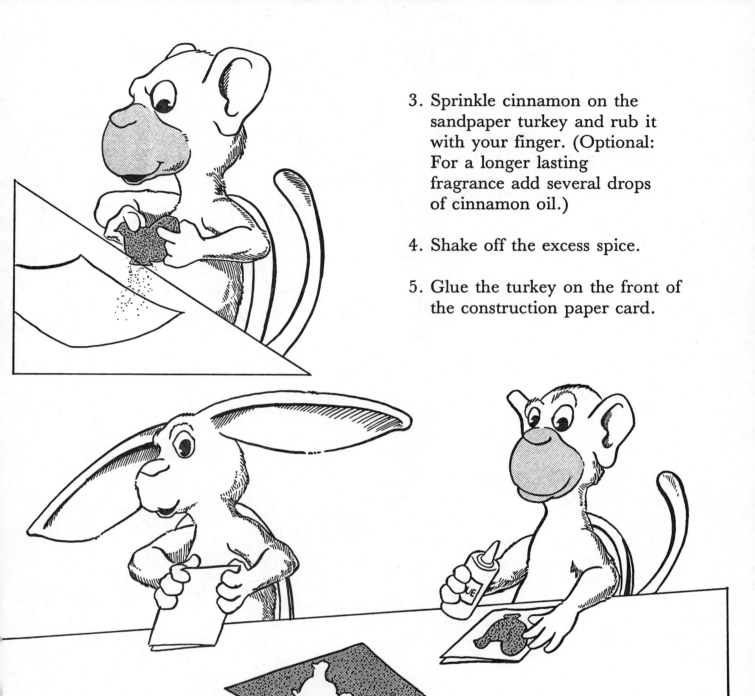

3. Sprinkle cinnamon on the sandpaper turkey and rub it with your finger. (Optional: For a longer lasting fragrance add several drops of cinnamon oil.)

4. Shake off the excess spice.

5. Glue the turkey on the front of the construction paper card.

6. Write your Thanksgiving message inside the card. (Here's a suggestion: ''Hope your Thanksgiving turkey tastes as good as it smells.'' Love, Bear) Put your card in an envelope, add a stamp, address, and mail it.

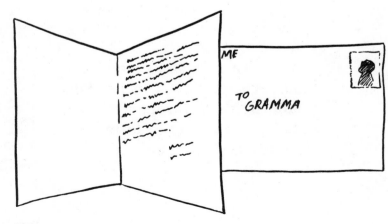

HALLOWEEN BAG

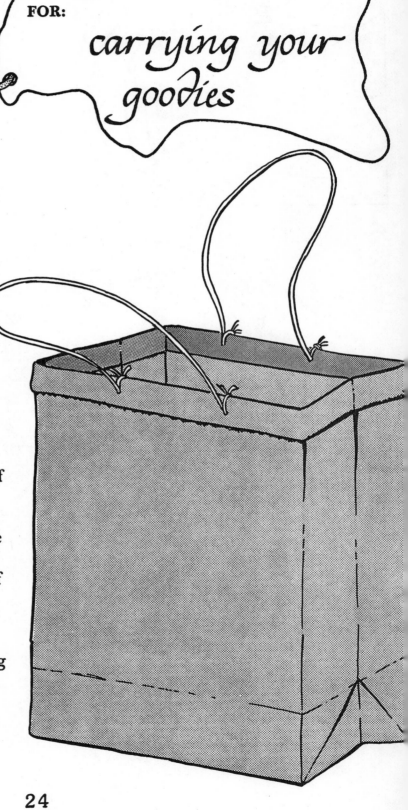

MATERIALS:

Grocery bag
Scissors
Duct tape
Paper punch
Brown twine
Piece of corrugated cardboard
Utility knife
Pencil
Water soluble printer's ink
Meat tray
Brayer

FOR:

carrying your goodies

TO MAKE:

1. Fold down the top edge of a grocery bag about two inches.

2. Put a piece of duct tape around the inside top edge of the bag.

3. Punch two holes, about three inches apart through the top edge of the front and back of the bag.

4. Cut two pieces of twine about twenty-four inches long and tie them through the holes in the bag to form the handles. (Use square knots.)

5. Using a utility knife, cut a piece of corrugated cardboard about the same size as one side of the grocery bag.

6. Draw a ghost on the corrugated cardboard leaving about a two inch border on all sides.

7. Cut around the ghost outline with a utility knife.

8. Using the utility knife, carefully peel back the top layer of paper revealing a ribbed ghost. Remove the excess paper so the ribs are clean.

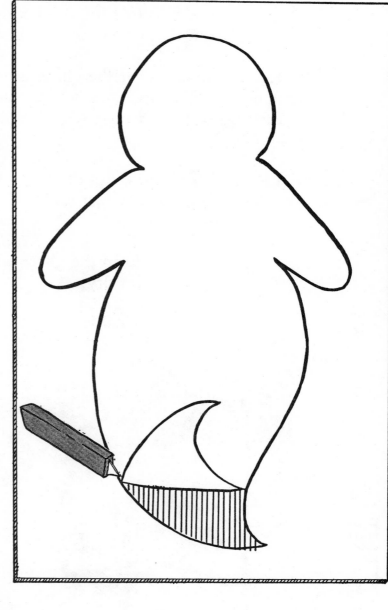

CAUTION: You only want to cut the top layer of paper.

9. Squirt some printer's ink on the meat tray and roll the ink out with a brayer until the brayer is covered with ink.

10. Roll the brayer over the ghost and its border. Re-ink the brayer as many times as necessary to coat the entire piece of corrugated cardboard. (Don't push too hard. You don't want to break the ribbing.)

11. Lay the inked ghost upside down on the grocery bag and rub firmly.

12. Lift up the ghost and let the print dry.

13. Repeat the printing process on the other side of the bag.

TURKEY ENVELOPE

MATERIALS:

Plastic tray
Finger paint
Brayer
9″ × 12″ envelope
Markers

FOR: *wrapping a seasonal gift*

TO MAKE:

1. Put a small amount of paint on a tray and smooth it out with a brayer.

2. Lay your hand in the paint and then on the envelope to make your handprint.

3. Repeat the handprinting process until the envelope is filled with prints. Let it dry.

4. Using markers, add turkey features to the handprints.

5. Use it to wrap your Thanksgiving napkins or another Fall gift.

PAINT

WINTER

FRAMED ART

MATERIALS:

Paint, crayons, pencils, or chalk
Any size paper
Lightweight posterboard
Scissors
Glue
Self-adhesive picture hooks

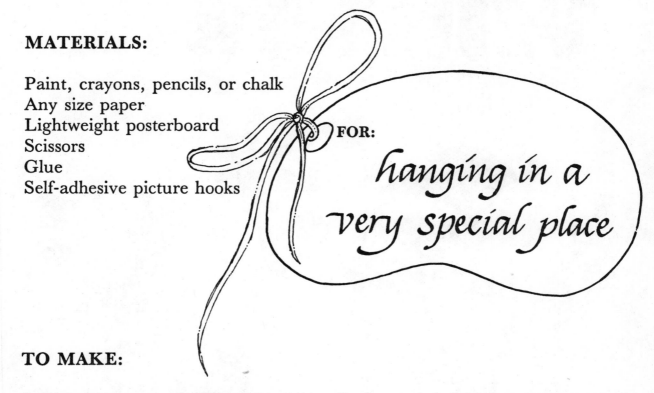

FOR: *hanging in a very special place*

TO MAKE:

1. Using crayons, chalk, paint, or pencils draw a picture that you would like to hang in your home.

2. Make a frame for your art:

   - Cut four strips of posterboard that are each two inches wide and eight inches longer than the sides of your artwork.

   - Trim the ends of each strip on a diagonal.

   - Glue the strips around the sides of the art so they overlap. Let the frame dry.

3. Tape the hooks to the top backside corners of your art. If it is a large piece of art also tape a hook in the center of the art.

DECORATED TISSUE BOX

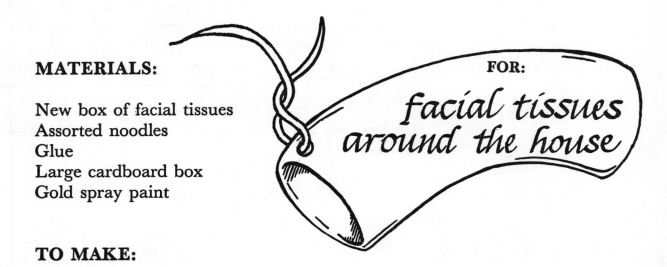

MATERIALS:

New box of facial tissues
Assorted noodles
Glue
Large cardboard box
Gold spray paint

FOR:

facial tissues around the house

TO MAKE:

1. Glue the noodles all over the sides and top of the unopened tissue box. Let it dry.

2. Put the tissue box into the large cardboard box and spray it gold.

3. Carefully take the tissue box out of the cardboard box. Let it dry.

4. Gently push in the perforation to open the box of tissues.

POINSETTIA CUP

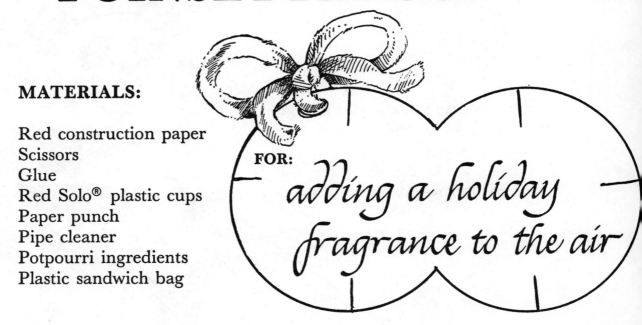

MATERIALS:

Red construction paper
Scissors
Glue
Red Solo® plastic cups
Paper punch
Pipe cleaner
Potpourri ingredients
Plastic sandwich bag

FOR: *adding a holiday fragrance to the air*

TO MAKE:

1. Cut two identical construction paper poinsettias between five and seven inches in diameter. (See illustration for two types of flowers.)

34

2. Fold up the petals of the top flower.

3. Glue the flowers together in the middle.

4. Glue the cup to the center of the flower.

5. Punch two holes opposite each other in the cup.

6. Secure the pipe cleaner through the holes to form a handle.

7. Put some of the 'potpourri' in a plastic bag and place it in the poinsettia cup.

POTPOURRI

Ingredients:

2 cups dried rose petals
2 cups crushed dried rosemary leaves
1 cup tiny pinecones
1T powdered oris root
1t crushed cloves
2t crushed cinnamon

Mix all of the above ingredients together in a large bowl and cover it. Let the mixture set for a week or so tossing it once or twice a day.

HOLIDAY DOLL

MATERIALS:

Styrofoam Christmas tree about 8'' high
Styrofoam ball about 2″ in diameter
Glue
Large mixing bowl
2 cups liquid starch
Piece of cotton fabric cut into a 25″ circle
Waxed paper
String
Piece of posterboard
Small box
Polyester fiberfill
Gold spray paint

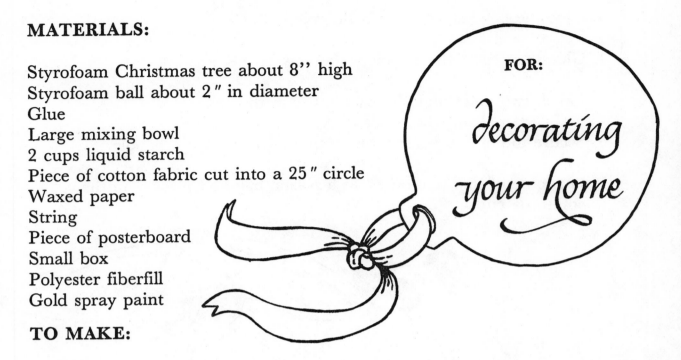

FOR:

decorating your home

TO MAKE:

1. Glue the styrofoam ball onto the top of the tree. Let it dry.

2. Pour the liquid starch into the mixing bowl.

3. Dip the cotton fabric into the liquid starch. Pull it out and gently squeeze the excess liquid from the fabric.

4. Sit the doll on a large piece of waxed paper. Having one person hold the styrofoam doll, drape the fabric over the styrofoam frame.

5. Shape the fabric around the neck and tie it with a piece of string to hold the fabric in place.

6. Shape the doll's gown any way you'd like. You might want to gather some of the fabric to the front to make it look like there are arms under the gown. Add a small piece of posterboard to represent a song book, a small box to be a gift, and so on. If necessary, secure these items with a drop of glue.

7. Using polyester fiberfill that has been dipped in starch shape the hair to fit the doll's head.

8. Let the doll dry overnight on the waxed paper.

9. Spray the entire doll gold. Let it dry. Carefully remove it from the waxed paper.

VALENTINE DOOR HANGING

MATERIALS:

Rectangular piece of white
   burlap to hang on the door
Red burlap
Marker
Scissors
Straight pins
Blunt-tipped needle
White and red rug yarn
Decorations for the hanging,
   such as sequins, ric-rac,
   glitter, etc.
Glue
¼ " dowel rod

wishing everyone 'Happy Valentine's Day'

FOR:

*Up and down
Up and down
But never all around!*

TO MAKE:

1. Draw a heart on the red burlap so it will
   fit on the piece of white burlap.

2. Cut the heart out. Pin it to the white burlap.

3. Using the blunt-tipped yarn needle and the white yarn, sew the heart
   onto the background. Say Mr. Aardvark's rhyme as you sew. Take out
   the pins.

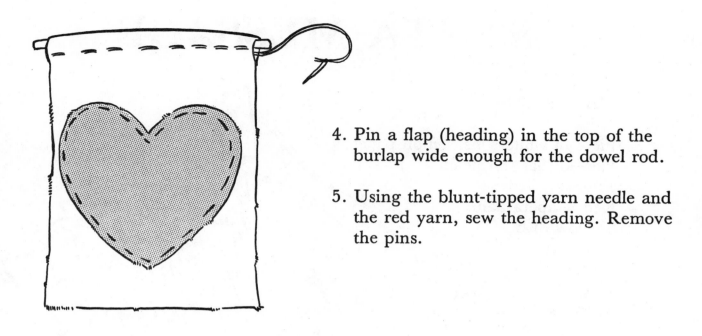

4. Pin a flap (heading) in the top of the burlap wide enough for the dowel rod.

5. Using the blunt-tipped yarn needle and the red yarn, sew the heading. Remove the pins.

6. Glue the decorations to your hanging. Let it dry.

7. Slip the dowel rod through the opening. Cut a piece of red rug yarn for the hanger. Tie it to each end of the dowel rod.

8. Hang it on your front door.

SANTA MESSAGE

MATERIALS:

Piece of white construction paper
Piece of flat styrofoam
Scissors
Red tempera paint
Shallow dish
Paint brush
Cotton
Glue
Markers

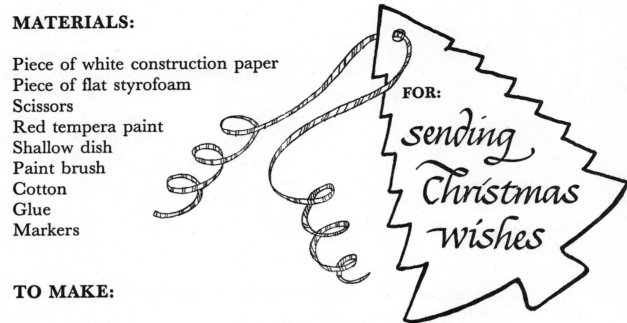

FOR:

sending Christmas wishes

TO MAKE:

1. Fold the construction paper in half forming a card.

2. Cut the piece of styrofoam into a long, narrow triangle about the length of your card.

3. Pour a little red paint into a shallow dish.

4. Paint the styrofoam triangle with red paint and print it on the card to form Santa's head and hat. Let it dry.

5. Form Santa's hat by gluing a cotton brim about two thirds of the way down the triangle and adding a cotton ball tassel at the top.

6. Draw Santa's face on the bottom third of the triangle. Using cotton create a beard.
   VARIATION: Create a Christmas tree from the triangle by using green paint and adding cotton ball ornaments.

7. Write your message on the inside.

BOOKMARK GREETING

MATERIALS:

Marker
Red, pink, and white
   construction paper
Scissors
Red ribbon about 10"-12"
   long and 1" wide
Glue

FOR:

*saying
I love you*

TO MAKE:

1. Draw six construction paper hearts about two and one half inches in diameter.

2. Carefully cut the hearts out.

3. Glue three of them on one side of the piece of ribbon.

4. Turn the ribbon over and glue the remaining hearts on the back of the first hearts. Let them dry.

5. Cut the ends of the ribbon in V-shapes.

6. Write a message on the hearts. (Here's a suggestion: "I Love You." One word on each heart.)

YOUR GIFT BAG

MATERIALS:

Large white plastic bag
Holiday stencils
Permanent markers
Heavy weight yarn

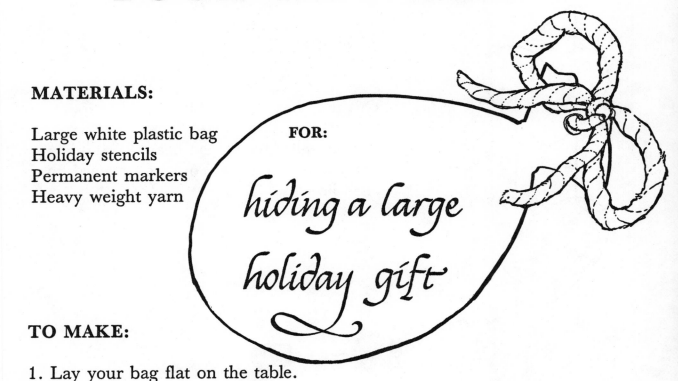

FOR: *hiding a large holiday gift*

TO MAKE:

1. Lay your bag flat on the table.

2. Decorate the bag by tracing around holiday stencils. Let the one side dry.
   VARIATION: Younger children might want to decorate their bags by drawing on them with markers.

3. Decorate the other side of the bag. Let it dry.

4. Carefully put your gift in the bag.

5. Tie the bag closed with a piece of colorful yarn.

HOLIDAY BASKET

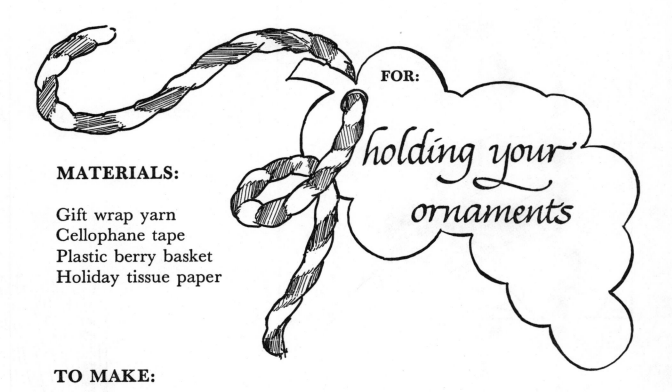

MATERIALS:

Gift wrap yarn
Cellophane tape
Plastic berry basket
Holiday tissue paper

FOR:

holding your ornaments

TO MAKE:

1. Cut a two foot piece of gift wrap yarn and wrap a piece of cellophane tape tightly around one end of it.

2. Tie the other end of the yarn to the basket.

3. Weave the yarn in and out of the spaces on the four sides of the basket. Tie a bow.

4. Cut and weave as many additional pieces of yarn as you would like. Tie each one off as you finish weaving a row.

5. When finished, cut a piece of tissue about thirty by fifteen inches. Fold it in half. Put your gift inside. Pull up the corners of the tissue paper. Tie them together with yarn. Set it in your basket.

ICE CREAM CONE ORNAMENT

FOR:

trimming your Christmas tree

MATERIALS:

Egg cartons
Sugar ice cream cones
Large marshmallows
2½ cups sifted powdered sugar
¼ t. cream of tartar
2 egg whites at room temperature

Food coloring
Mixing bowl
Electric beater
Table knife
Red cinnamon candies
Multi-colored decorettes
Long Christmas tree hooks

TO MAKE:

1. Turn the egg carton upside down and poke a hole through each egg cup to set your ice cream cones in.

2. Break away pieces from the top of each cone until the cone is about three inches tall. Set the cones in the egg carton.

3. Mold two marshmallows together so they look like a scoop of ice cream. Place each 'scoop' in an ice cream cone.

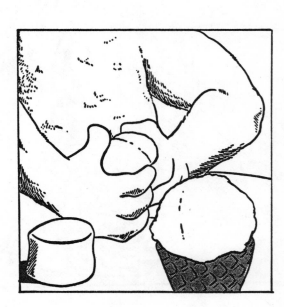

48

Don't make the icing until you're ready to put it on the ice cream cones.

Make the sugar icing: Place the sugar, cream of tartar, egg whites, and food coloring in a small mixing bowl. Blend at a low speed with an electric beater, occasionally scraping the sides of the bowl. Turn the mixer to a higher speed and beat until the icing is very stiff. (A knife drawn through the icing should make a clean path. Add a little more sugar if the icing does not become stiff in about 4 or 5 minutes.) Makes enough icing for about one dozen ice cream cones.

4. Using the table knife spread the icing over the marshmallows and down over the edges of the cones.

5. Decorate the icing with cinnamon candies or multi-colored decorettes.

6. Set the ice cream cones back in the egg carton and poke Christmas tree hooks down through the icing into the marshmallows.

7. Let them dry overnight before hanging them on the tree.

PINECONE ANGEL
ORNAMENT

MATERIALS:

3″ pinecone
Gold cord
1 small nut in a shell
Black fine tip marker
2″ dried milkweed pod
Glue

FOR:

celebrating Jesus' birth

TO MAKE:

1. Break or snip out the top petals of the pinecone to make a place for the angel's head.

2. Wrap the cord under the next layer of pinecone petals to form the hanger.

50

3. Draw facial features on the nut.

4. Glue the nut to the top of the pinecone. Let it dry.

5. Take the milkweed pod, open it, and remove the seeds. Push the pod, hollow side facing forward, into the back of the pinecone to form the wings. Glue and let dry.

STARBURST ORNAMENT

MATERIALS:

Waxed paper
Posterboard
Scissors
Small paint brush
Glue
Colored wooden toothpicks
Colored cord

FOR: adding a burst of color to your Christmas tree

TO MAKE:

1. Place a piece of waxed paper on your work surface.

2. Cut two one and a half inch circles from the posterboard.

3. Place a posterboard circle on the waxed paper and paint it with glue.

4. Place toothpicks in a starburst arrangement on the posterboard circle.

5. Form a cord hanger and place it in the glue along with the toothpicks.

6. Paint a second posterboard circle with glue and place it on the top of the toothpicks and cord.

7. Cover the ornament with a second piece of waxed paper and set something heavy on top of it until the glue has thoroughly dried.

8. Carefully remove the waxed paper and hang the ornament on your Christmas tree.

SPRING

EASTER EGG SUNCATCHER

MATERIALS:

Metal hanger
Brightly colored pastel tissue paper
Liquid starch
Small container
Waxed paper
Scissors
Crepe paper streamers

FOR: *letting the sunshine through*

TO MAKE:

1. Bend the hanger into an egg shape.

2. Tear the various colors of tissue paper into strips about four to six inches long.

3. Pour the liquid starch into a small container.

4. Lay a piece of waxed paper on the table to work on.

5. Lay a large piece of tissue paper that is slightly larger than the hanger on the waxed paper.

6. Put the hanger on the tissue paper.

7. Take one of the strips of tissue paper and lay it on the hanger. Dip your finger into the starch and spread the starch all over the paper strip so it sticks. Take another piece of tissue, lay it next to the first one, and spread starch on it. Continue this process until the entire rim of the hanger is layered with colored tissue. Add more tissue strips to the middle of the hanger. Let the suncatcher dry.

8. Trim around the hanger to form the egg shape.

9. Tie a crepe paper bow on the top of the hanger.

10. Hang it in a sunny window.

CINNAMON AIR FRESHENER

MATERIALS:

8T cinnamon
6T applesauce
Small bowl
Spoon
Waxed paper
Rolling pin
Medium size cookie cutters
Rounded toothpicks
Cake drying rack
Narrow ribbon

FOR:

making the kitchen smell good

TO MAKE:

1. Combine the cinnamon and the applesauce in a bowl. Mix with a spoon. Knead and form into two balls. If it is too dry, add a little more applesauce and knead again.

2. Place a piece of waxed paper on your work surface and sprinkle it with cinnamon.

3. Roll out your dough on the waxed paper until it is no thinner than one quarter inch.

4. Using cookie cutters cut shapes out of the dough. (Makes 10-12)

5. Using the toothpick, punch a hole near the top of each shape so a narrow ribbon can be tied through it.

6. Place cut outs on the cake racks and dry them in a 150° oven for three to four hours.

7. Finish by adding a ribbon to the air fresheners so they can easily be hung up.

EGG CARTON GARDEN

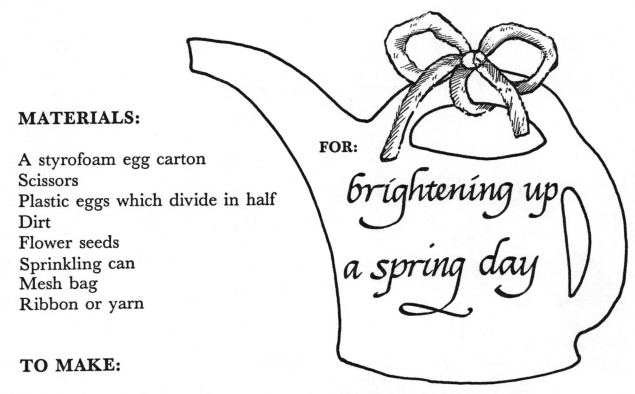

MATERIALS:

A styrofoam egg carton
Scissors
Plastic eggs which divide in half
Dirt
Flower seeds
Sprinkling can
Mesh bag
Ribbon or yarn

FOR:

brightening up

a spring day

TO MAKE:

1. Cut a four or six section piece off of your egg carton.

2. Put half of a plastic egg in each section.

3. Fill each plastic egg-half with dirt.

4. Add a few flower seeds to each one.

5. Water your newly planted seeds.

6. Cover the planted seeds with the other halves of the plastic eggs. These will act like small greenhouses.

7. Carefully slide the planted seeds into a mesh bag and tie it with a bow.

8. Add a tag that tells how to care for the seeds.

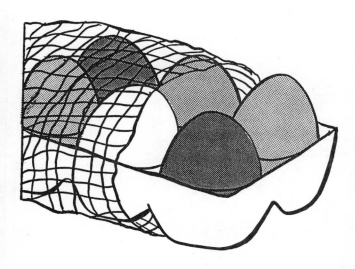

CARE INSTRUCTIONS

* Place the garden in a warm place.

* When sprouts appear, remove the top of the eggs and put them in a sunny window.

* Keep the soil moist.

* Transplant the seedlings in your garden.

BUTTERFLY MAGNET

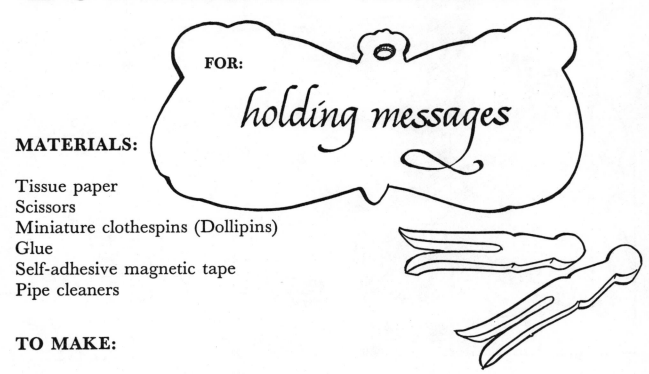

FOR: *holding messages*

MATERIALS:

Tissue paper
Scissors
Miniature clothespins (Dollipins)
Glue
Self-adhesive magnetic tape
Pipe cleaners

TO MAKE:

1. Cut three pieces of tissue paper approximately three inches square.

2. Take a piece of tissue paper, gather it in the middle, and push it in the clothespin. Repeat the process for the other two pieces of tissue. Put several drops of glue between the prongs of the clothespins to hold the tissue paper in place.

3. Cut a piece of magnetic tape that is the same width and about two-thirds of the length of the clothespin. Attach it to the clothespin.

4. Twist a small piece of pipe cleaner around the top of the clothespin to form the butterfly's antennae.

SPRING WREATH

MATERIALS:

Piece of cardboard about 8″ square
Scissors
Several remnants of lightweight cotton fabric
Liquid starch
Small bowl
2 styrofoam egg cartons
Medium size doilies
Glue

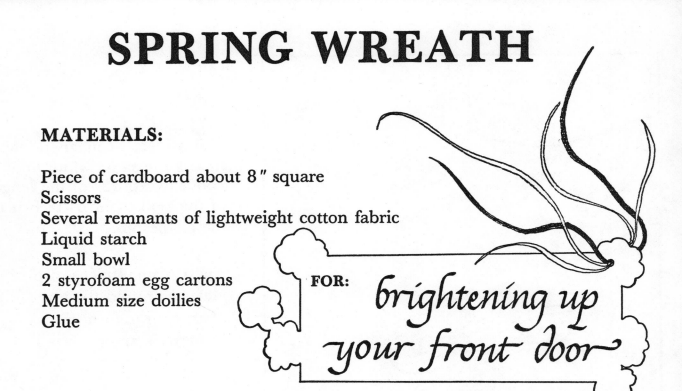

FOR: *brightening up your front door*

TO MAKE:

1. Cut the cardboard into a circle. Cut the center out to make a wreath.

2. Cut eighteen three inch squares out of the fabric.

3. Pour starch into the bowl.

4. Dip each fabric square into the starch. Wipe the excess starch from the piece and mold it into one of the egg sections to form a blossom. Let all of the blossoms dry overnight.

5. Glue the paper doilies onto the cardboard circle.

6. Pop the fabric blossoms out of the carton and glue them around the wreath. Let the wreath dry.

7. Hang it on your door.

EASTER EGG CARD

MATERIALS:

Pastel colored construction paper
Fine sandpaper
Scissors
Crayons
Glue
Electric iron
Newsprint
Marker

FOR:
wishing you a 'Happy Easter'

TO MAKE:

1. Fold the construction paper in half to form a card.

2. Cut an egg shape from the piece of fine sandpaper that will fit on the card.

3. Pressing hard with the crayons, color the entire egg.

4. Glue the egg to the inside left-hand page of the card. Let it dry.

5. Turn the iron on a warm setting.

6. Make an ironing pad by placing a stack of newsprint on your table.

7. Close the card. Cover it with a piece of clean newsprint.

8. Iron the card so that the sandpaper egg prints on the inside right-hand page of the card.

9. Write an Easter message on the front of the card.

HANDPRINT CARD

MATERIALS:

Construction paper
Tempera paint
Pie pan
Scissors
Pencil

FOR: remembering how small I once was

TO MAKE:

1. Fold the piece of construction paper in half to form a card.

2. Pour enough tempera paint in the pie pan to cover the bottom.

3. Lay the flat of your hand in the paint.

4. Take your hand out of the paint and make your handprint on the front of the card with your thumb or small finger along the folded edge. Let it dry.

5. Leaving the card folded, cut out your handprint so the card is now in the shape of your hand.

6. Open up the card and write your message.

BUNNY BASKET

MATERIALS:

Paper plates
Stapler
Scissors
Cotton
Glue
Pieces and scraps of construction paper
Fine tip marker

FOR: *carrying special surprises*

TO MAKE:

1. Fold the paper plate in half so the top side of the plate is on the inside. Staple the corners (not the top) closed.

2. Beginning near the center top of the plate, cut the bunny's ears.

3. Fluff the cotton and glue it on both sides of the ears and at the back for the bunny tail.

4. Cut pieces of construction paper for the bunny's eyes and nose. Glue them on. Draw a mouth.

5. Cut a rectangular handle about ten inches long and an inch wide. Fold it, put the ends inside the paper plate near the top, and staple them to each side.

6. Slip the gift inside. Staple the bunny closed if necessary.

TULIP TISSUE PAPER

FOR:

wrapping a Spring gift

MATERIALS:

Marker
Corrugated cardboard
Utility knife
Glue
Tissue paper
Tempera paint
Paint brush

TO MAKE:

1. Draw two tulip shapes about three inches high on the corrugated board.

2. Using the utility knife, cut out the two tulips.

3. To make the tulip easier to hold, glue the two tulips together. Let it dry.

4. Again using the knife, carefully peel the top layer of paper off one tulip revealing the ribbed inner layer. Clean out the ribbings to get a more detailed print.

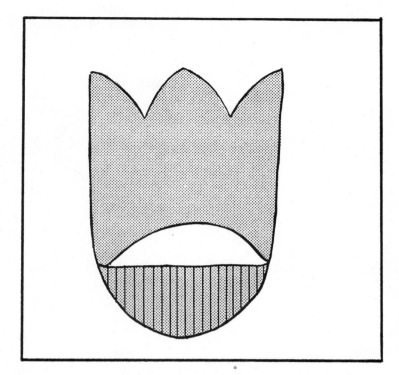

5. Lay the piece of tissue paper on the table.

6. Paint the tulip with tempera paint.

7. Print several tulip shapes on the tissue paper. Paint the tulip again and make several more prints. Continue until the tissue paper is full of spring flowers. Let the paper dry.

NOTE CARDS

FOR:

writing to special people

MATERIALS:

Miniature cookie cutters
Gum erasers
Typing paper
Envelopes
Scissors
Paper towels
2 small meat trays
Tempera paint
Brayer

Meat tray slightly
    larger than the envelopes
Ribbon

TO MAKE:

1. Select the miniature cookie cutter you want. Lay it on top of the eraser and press down firmly to cut through the eraser.

2. Cut a piece of typing paper the length of your envelope and twice as wide. Fold it in half to form a note card.

"The paper towel needs to be thoroughly soaked but not soggy."

3. Make a stamp pad:
   - Cut two or three pieces of paper towel to fit in the meat tray.
   - Pour a little tempera paint on the paper towels and spread it out with a brayer.

4. Press the eraser on the stamp pad and then on the the note card to print the design. Repeat this process as many times as desired. Set the note card aside to dry.

5. Repeat the printing process on the back flap of the envelope. Set it aside to dry.

6. Print as many cards and envelopes as you wish.

7. Package the note cards and envelopes by placing them on a meat tray and securing them in place with a ribbon.

77

FABRIC HANGING

FOR:

saving your drawing

MATERIALS:

1 piece of 11″ × 18″ solid color cloth sheet
Paper towel roll
Glue
Twine
Fabric crayons
Typing paper
Stack of newsprint
Electric iron

TO MAKE:

1. Glue one end of the fabric around the paper towel roll.

2. String a piece of twine through the roll. Knot it at the top to form the hanger.

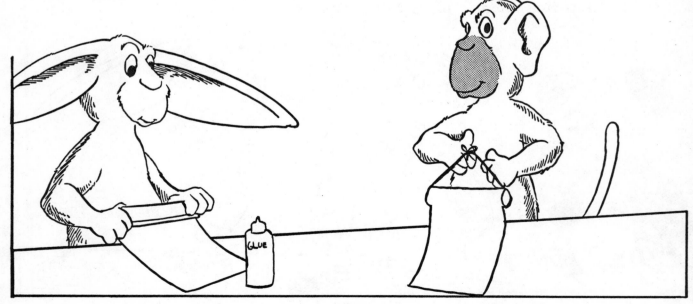

3. Color a picture on a piece of typing paper.

4. Turn the iron on to the setting designated on your crayons.

5. Make an ironing pad by placing a stack of newsprint on your table.

6. Transfer the picture to the fabric by following the ironing instructions on the box of crayons.

PINWHEEL WREATH

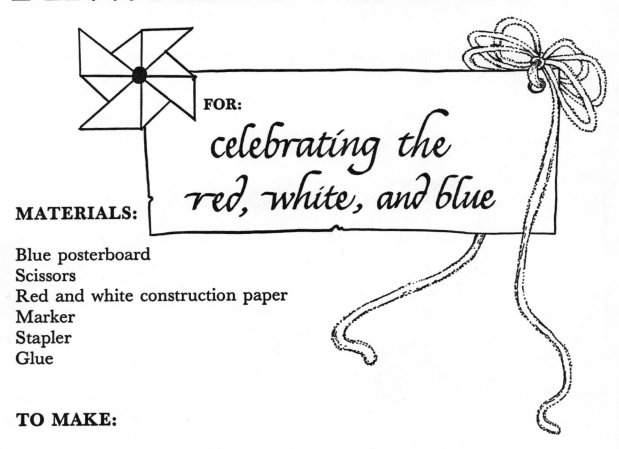

FOR:

celebrating the red, white, and blue

MATERIALS:

Blue posterboard
Scissors
Red and white construction paper
Marker
Stapler
Glue

TO MAKE:

1. Cut a posterboard circle eight inches in diameter.

2. Cut four red and four white five by five inch squares from the construction paper.

3. Draw a one inch diameter circle in the center of each square.

4. Cut straight lines from the corners of each square to the edge of the circle.

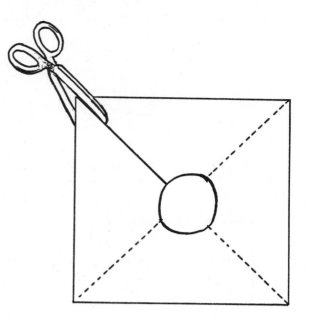

5. Fold half of each corner to the center of the circle and staple to form a pinwheel. Do this for all eight squares.

6. Glue the pinwheels around the posterboard circle.

7. Cut small red or white circles and glue them to the center of each pinwheel.

GINGERBREAD MESSAGE

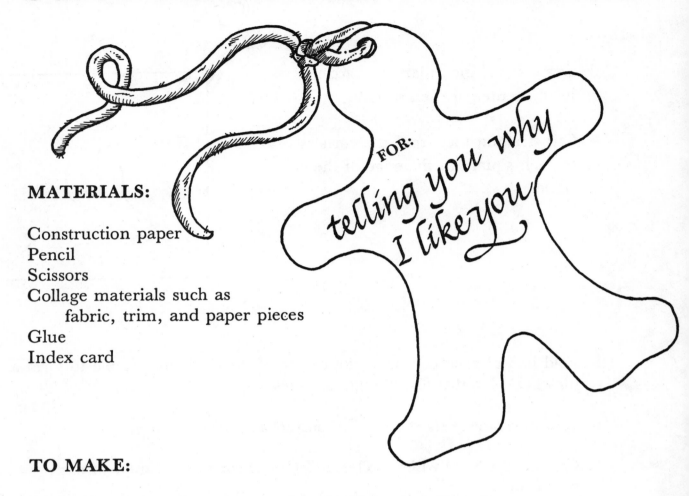

FOR:

telling you why I like you

MATERIALS:

Construction paper
Pencil
Scissors
Collage materials such as
    fabric, trim, and paper pieces
Glue
Index card

TO MAKE:

1. Decide who you're going to give the gingerbread card to.

2. Draw a large gingerbread shape on the construction paper.

3. Cut it out.

4. Close your eyes and picture the person you're going to give the card to.

5. After you have thought for awhile, open your eyes. Using the collage materials dress the character to look like the person receiving the card.

6. Give the index card and pencil to a friend who can write. Tell your friend what you like about the person receiving the card. Your friend should write down what you say. Attach the card to the leg or hand of the gingerbread character.

FOURTH OF JULY BANNER

FOR: *wishing your neighborhood a 'Happy Fourth of July'*

MATERIALS:

A solid color outdoor banner cloth (Buy in an art store.)
Red, blue, green, and yellow permanent markers
Black spray paint
4-5 wooden stakes about 4' long
Hammer
Thumbtacks

TO MAKE:

1. Lay the banner cloth on the floor. Lay a tray of markers near the cloth.

2. Let the children color a variety of sizes and colors of fireworks on the cloth. Let it dry.

3. Carry it outside. Lay it flat on the ground. Paint "HAPPY 4th" across the middle of the banner. Let it dry.

4. Hammer the stakes into the ground where you want to display the banner.

5. Tack the banner to the stakes.

6. Have fun watching all of the people read your holiday greeting.

WOVEN BASKET

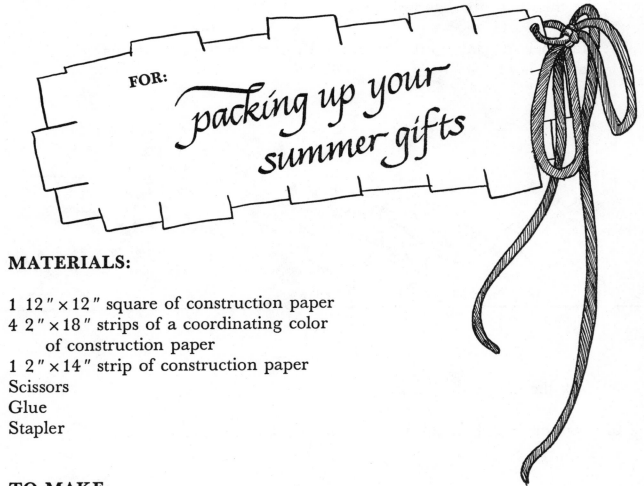

FOR: *packing up your summer gifts*

MATERIALS:

1 12″×12″ square of construction paper
4 2″×18″ strips of a coordinating color
    of construction paper
1 2″×14″ strip of construction paper
Scissors
Glue
Stapler

TO MAKE:

1. Fold the square in half and cut slits from the fold every two inches, stopping each slit about two inches from the edge of the paper. Open the square.

2. Weave the four eighteen inch strips in and out of the slits remembering to alternate when you start weaving each row.

3. Glue the ends of the strips down, let them dry, and then trim.

4. Form the basket by bringing the diagonal corners together. Add a handle by inserting the short strip between the two corners and stapling it closed.

FOURTH OF JULY WRAP

FOR: *keeping your present a secret*

MATERIALS:

Red and blue tempera paint
2 styrofoam meat trays
White tissue paper
Different sizes of star-shaped cookie cutters

TO MAKE:

1. Pour a small amount of red tempera paint into one meat tray and a small amount of blue tempera into the other one.

2. Lay a piece of tissue paper on the table.

3. Dip a cookie cutter into the tempera paint and then print it onto the tissue paper. Repeat this process with different sizes of cookie cutters and colors of paint until the tissue is filled with stars.

4. Let the paper dry.

5. Wrap your pinwheel wreath that you have previously made.

89

LOOK WHAT ELSE .....

FALL IDEAS

Fall Wreath

1. Cut the base for the wreath and make the fabric blossoms out of fall colors the same as you did for the Spring Wreath on page 64.

2. You'll also need a package of gold doilies. Take a doily, gather it in the middle, and glue it to the base of the wreath. Continue in this manner gluing doilies around the entire wreath.

3. Glue a fabric blossom in the center of each doily.

4. Let it dry.

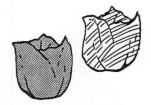

Refrigerator Magnets

1. Make the dough using the same recipe as you did for the Cinnamon Air Freshener on page 58.

2. Cut out appropriate shapes but do not poke a hole in them.

3. Dry as instructed.

4. Glue pieces of magnetic tape to the backs of the cinnamon shapes and use them as refrigerator magnets.

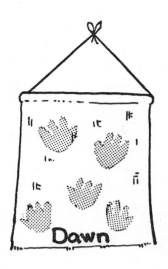

Handprint Hanging

1. Make the fabric background the same way you did for the Fabric Hanging on page 78.

2. Spread water soluble printer's ink on a tray using a brayer.

3. Lay your hands in the ink and print them on the fabric.

4. Let dry.

5. Using a marker write your name under your handprints.

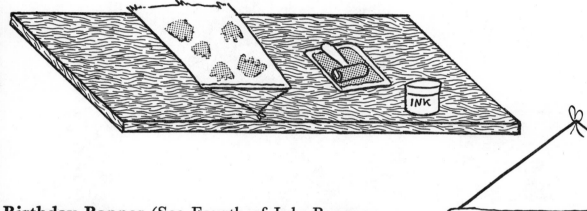

Birthday Banner (See Fourth of July Banner on page 84.)

1. If you are going to hang this banner inside, get indoor banner cloth from the art supply store.

2. Position the banner vertically. Using permanent markers draw a large bouquet of balloons on the banner. Write the date of everyone's birthday on separate balloons. Color the rest of them.

3. Draw strings from each balloon which gather at the bottom of the banner.

4. Hang the banner on the door whenever someone is celebrating a birthday.

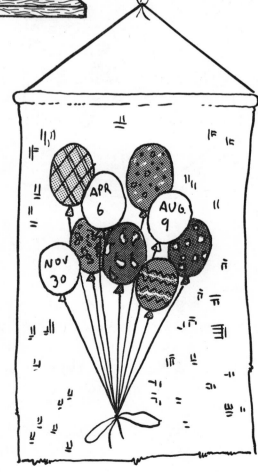

93

WINTER IDEAS

Memo Pad

1. Cut typing paper into memo pad size pieces about 4"x5½" or 3"x11".

2. Print winter shapes on the papers using the same procedure as you did for the Note Cards on page 76.

3. To form the memo pad:
   — Pour a little bit of 'padding compound' (found in an office supply store) on a meat tray.
   — Stack the papers carefully together.
   — Clip them together with paper clips on each side near the top.
   — Dip the top of the pad into the compound.
   — Let it dry.

Pinwheel Christmas Tree

1. Cut a triangle shaped Christmas tree out of green posterboard.

2. Make red and white or red and green pinwheels using the same procedure as you did for the Pinwheel Wreath on page 80.

3. Glue the pinwheels on the Christmas tree shape and glue a small red or white circle to the center of each pinwheel.

4. Hang it on the front door for the Christmas season.

Potpourri Ornaments

1. Prepare the potpourri recipe on page 35 omitting the pinecones.

2. Poke pipe cleaner hangers into small styrofoam balls, bells, or wreaths.

3. Cover the ornaments with white glue.

4. Roll them in the potpourri mixture.

5. Let them dry.

6. Hang them on the Christmas tree.

Shining Ornaments

1. Color your coffee filters using the same procedure as you did for the Fall Suncatcher on page 12.

2. Lay the filters out flat and paint one side of them with Mod Podge®. Let them dry and paint the other side.

3. Trace stars, bells, candy canes, and Christmas trees on the filters. Cut the shapes out.

4. Punch holes in the tops of the ornaments and add colorful ribbon hangers.

5. Hang them on the Christmas tree.

Holiday Mobile

1. Make stuffed candles, Christmas trees, bells, or candy canes following the same procedure as you used for the Jack-O-Lantern Hanging on page 16.

2. Attach a ribbon loop to the top of each one and hang the shapes from the ceiling or doorway.

3. Try hanging two or three together in chain fashion.

Valentine Greeting

1. Fold a piece of red construction paper into a card.

2. Glue a Valentine doily to the front of the card.

3. Make a sandpaper cinnamon heart the same way as you did the turkey in the Thanksgiving Card on page 22.

4. Glue the heart in the center of the doily.

5. Write a Valentine message inside the card.

SPRING IDEAS

Daffodil Basket

1. Change the poinsettia on page 34 into a daffodil by using yellow Solo® cups and cutting yellow construction paper flowers.

2. Convert the potpourri on page 35 to a spring mixture by replacing the pine cones with dried yellow flower petals such as marigolds.

3. Give for May Day or Mother's Day.

Seed Packet (See Turkey Envelope on page 27.)

1. Create a ladybug envelope by making red thumb prints (use a red stamp pad) on a white letter-size envelope. Decorate the prints with black dots.

2. Place some flower seeds and planting instructions inside the envelope.

3. Give as a "Welcome Spring" gift.

Spring Ducks

1. Prepare the same mixture as you did for the Pumpkin Soaps on page 14 except, add only yellow food coloring to the water.

2. Mold the soap mixture into duck shapes and give them as an Easter gift, Mother's Day present, or Spring surprise. They float, so you might suggest that the person have fun with them in the bathtub.

SUMMER IDEAS

Holiday Sacks

1. Prepare the top of a brown, white or pastel colored lunch bag in the same way as you did the Halloween Bag on page 24.

2. Draw a heart, flower, gingerbread man, duck or design of your choice on an appropriate size piece of corrugated cardboard.

3. Cut around the design the same way you did the ghost.

4. Print the design on both sides of the lunch bag.

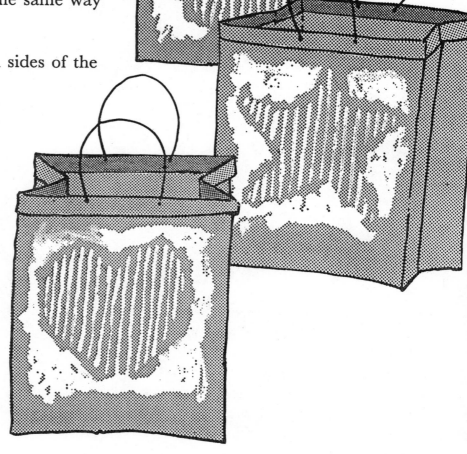

Summer Bookmark

1. Draw and cut out six construction paper flowers, stars, suns or shapes of your choice.

2. Glue them on appropriately colored ribbon in the same way as you did the hearts for the Bookmark Greeting on page 42.

99

FOR EVERY MONTH

an important resource for child care professionals

TAKE A LOOK AT BUILDING BLOCKS NEWSPAPER

PUBLISHED:
10 times a year with expanded editions in November/December and May/June.

RATES:
Family Edition: $10.00
Child Care Edition: $15.00

FOR A SAMPLE ISSUE SEND YOUR NAME, ADDRESS (INCLUDING ZIP CODE) AND $2.00 TO:

BUILDING BLOCKS
38W567 Brindlewood
Elgin, Illinois 60123

CHILD CARE EDITION

BUILDING BLOCKS **Child Care Edition** offers early childhood professionals a total curriculum resource. It is divided into two parts. The first part is a potpourri of monthly ideas, activities, and information for you to use in your classroom as well as share with your parents. It is hand-lettered and charmingly illustrated.

The second part of the **Child Care Edition** features a different unit each issue. Included in each unit are:

- LEARNING CENTER SUGGESTIONS
- CIRCLE TIME ACTIVITIES
- ART IDEAS
- MUSIC, FINGERPLAYS AND ACTIVE GAMES
- EASY RECIPES
- ROUTINE TIME ACTIVITIES

BUILDING BLOCKS also offers a **Family Edition** which consists of the hand-lettered and illustrated portion.

The Circle Time Book

by Liz and Dick Wilmes

The Circle Time Book captures the spirit of seasons and holidays. The big book is filled with more than 400 circle time activities for the preschool classroom. Thirty-nine seasons and holidays are included.

A useful companion to **Everyday Circle Times.**

ISBN 0-943452-00-7, Building Blocks, 128 pages $8.95

Everyday Circle Times

by Liz and Dick Wilmes

Over 900 ideas for Circle Time. This is one of the most important and challenging periods in the children's day. Choose activities from 48 different units. Each unit is introduced with an opening activity, and expanded through language and active games, fingerplays, stores, recipes, books and more.

ISBN 0-943452-01-5, Building Blocks, 216 pages $12.95

Felt Board Fun

by Liz and Dick Wilmes

Make your felt board come alive. Discover how versatile it is as the children become involved with the wide range of activities designed to help them think creatively and learn basic concepts.

This unique book contains over 150 ideas with accompanying patterns.

ISBN 0-943452-02-3, Building Blocks, 224 pages $12.95

Imagination Stretchers

by Liz and Dick Wilmes

Have fun as you help your children learn to think creatively, use their past experiences, develop language, and enjoy sharing ideas. Choose from over 400 conversation starters designed to encourage each child to express his/her feelings, thoughts and opinions on a wide variety of topics.

ISBN 0-943452-04-X, Building Blocks, 88 pages $6.95

Parachute Play

by Liz and Dick Wilmes

Now a year-round approach to one of the most versatile pieces of large muscle equipment. Starting with the basic techniques, **Parachute Play** provides you with over one hundred activities to make your parachute or a large bed sheet come alive for the children in your group.

ISBN 0-943452-03-1, Building Blocks, 96 pages $7.95

Exploring Art

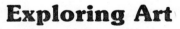

by Liz and Dick Wilmes

Create it — Display it — Enjoy it — the secret to enhancing your children's art experience. **Exploring Art** features a variety of easy art activities for each month. Every idea is coordinated with an introductory activity, a display suggestion, and extension activities for expanding art into the curriculum. Over 250 art ideas in all, along with more than 500 related activities.

ISBN 0-943452-05-8, Building Blocks, 256 pages $16.95

Classroom Parties

by Susan Spaete

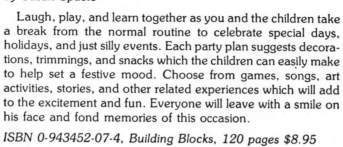

Laugh, play, and learn together as you and the children take a break from the normal routine to celebrate special days, holidays, and just silly events. Each party plan suggests decorations, trimmings, and snacks which the children can easily make to help set a festive mood. Choose from games, songs, art activities, stories, and other related experiences which will add to the excitement and fun. Everyone will leave with a smile on his face and fond memories of this occasion.

ISBN 0-943452-07-4, Building Blocks, 120 pages $8.95

Parent Programs and Open Houses

by Susan Spaete

Parent Programs and Open Houses is filled with a wide variety of year 'round presentations, pre-registration ideas, open houses, and end-of-the-year gatherings. Each of the programs involve the children from the beginning planning stages through the actual event. They are simple, short, and child-centered. Try them. Everyone will have a good time!

ISBN 0-943452-08-2, Building Blocks, 152 pages $9.95

ORDER FORM

	QTY		EACH	TOTAL
NAME _____	_____	THE CIRCLE TIME BOOK	$ 8.95	_____
	_____	EVERYDAY CIRCLE TIMES	$12.95	_____
ADDRESS _____	_____	FELT BOARD FUN	$12.95	_____
	_____	EXPLORING ART	$16.95	_____
CITY _____	_____	IMAGINATION STRETCHERS	$ 6.95	_____
	_____	PARACHUTE PLAY	$ 7.95	_____
STATE _____ ZIP _____	_____	GIFTS, CARDS & WRAPS	$ 7.95	_____
	_____	CLASSROOM PARTIES	$ 8.95	_____
	_____	PARENT PROGRAM & OPEN HOUSES	$ 9.95	_____
		TOTAL		_____

AVAILABLE FROM BOOKSTORES, SCHOOL SUPPLY STORES
OR ORDER DIRECTLY FROM:

38W567 Brindlewood, Elgin, Illinois 60123
312-742-1013   800-233-2448